CAGED:

A Teenager's Guide Book To Coming Out As LGBTQ+ To Parents

Kevin M. Cook

Caged: A Teenager's Guide Book To Coming Out As LGBTQ+ To Parents

Self-Orientation (Chapter 1)

Coming out can be frightening, but it's important to remember that you are in control of your journey. Come out to your friends, family, and community when it is safe for you to do so

Coming out to someone tough and rigid can be discouraging. Relax and recognize that being nervous is normal. Stay strong! Above all, regardless of how others respond or react to your news, love and admire yourself.

Understanding and acknowledging

Knowing and understanding your reasons for coming out is critical, and this is the first step toward answering questions and dispelling doubts.

People come out for a variety of reasons, the most common of which are:

They are ready to start dating and want to inform close friends and family members.

They do not want others making assumptions about them or gossiping about them.

They are bored of hearing other individuals employ negative marker concepts.

They feel that they're living in a taradiddle or aren't being genuine to themselves, and they want to be recognized for who they are.

Fears

There are several reasons why individuals opt not to come out, just as there are numerous reasons why they wish to come out, and here are some of the probable causes of their anxieties;

They are unsure of who they are or how they feel. They are also attempting to determine the impacts for themselves.

They're hilarious. They will be subjected to bullying, impunity, demarcation, and even violence.

Their family, friends, and community are unaware, and they are concerned about what may happen if others establish up there.

They reside in a community that has not been open to LGBTQ persons.

Considerations in Chapter 2

Before coming out, it is important to observe and evaluate several repercussions and potential outcomes. These results are of many possibilities, but what matters is that some are frequent and may be used as a guide to coming out. Some frequent points to consider are:

First reactions might alter.

Whether your parents suspect anything or not, this is the first time they are receiving this news. You've had months, if not years, to come to terms with it and be ready to participate. They are still in the process of being set up, so keep in mind that early replies aren't always permanent, and they will need time to utilize this information.

Self-convenience is essential.

When determining whether or not to come out to your parents, you must analyze your circumstances.

What is appropriate for one individual may not be appropriate for another. Always prioritize your safety and well-being.

You have choices.

You don't have to tell them all at once if you're more concerned about telling one of them.

Begin with the parent with whom you feel most comfortable speaking. Trust your intuition about whether it's preferable to inform them separately or collectively.

It is critical to maintaining one's privacy and rest of mind.

This one is easy to ignore since you'll be so glad when you finally tell them that it's natural to forget to be specific about what you want to do next. Decide ahead of time whether you want them to share the news of your coming out with your family or if you want it kept between you for the time being - and be clear about it.

Their approval or authorization is not required.

Try not to expect too much from your parents, and avoid gauging the success of the talk by their first answer if possible.

But don't despair or quit if it's not what you expected. They may just need more time. It's not about them. It's all about you and owning yourself. Demonstrate that you're still the same person they've always liked, but more honest.

Questions are welcome.

One source of anxiety is a barrage of inquiries, particularly when knowing the answers might be difficult and uncomfortable. Don't stress yourself out by attempting to predict every response ahead of time.

Questions from your parents are normal (but don't feel obligated to answer effects you don't agree with), and whether you have answers or not, be as honest as possible.

Chapter 3: The Beginning (Forming a support system)

Informing a Reliable Friend

Choose a supportive companion who will assist you in gaining confidence. An open-minded and sympathetic companion might help you obtain the strength to go ahead.

If your first experience coming out to someone is favorable, you may be less afraid of informing others in the future.

It may be simpler for you to come out to your friends before notifying your family. Also, remember that you are in command. However, if you feel more comfortable informing your parents first, that is the route you should pursue.

Remember that individuals do not always meet your expectations, and you cannot control anyone's reaction. Don't be disheartened if someone you inform does not respond as you expected.

People are often astonished or scared at first, but they become more tolerant after some time has passed.

Sequestration

Choose a relaxing, private setting to inform them. While there is no perfect way to come out, a quiet, distraction-free time and location may help.

When you or your companion is upset, nervous, or busy, avoid having a debate. That way, you'll be able to communicate yourself more readily, and your buddy will be able to reuse what you've said.

You wouldn't want to break the news to a buddy who has a basketball game in 10 minutes or is rushing late for work.

You don't need to make a huge deal out of it. Simply invite your buddy to hang together and explain that you have a commodity to share with them.

Honesty

Try to be straightforward, factual, and upbeat. "I wanted to tell you about a secret, I'm homosexual, and I'm telling you because I trust you and know you'll be there for me," take a deep breath and say.

If you haven't informed anybody else, tell your buddy that this is the first time you've told anyone and that you decided to tell them because you know they'll be there for you.

While it is a significant moment, it is not the same as confessing to a crime or alerting a buddy that you have a life-changing illness. You're having a conversation with someone you trust. Remember that this is a wonderful, fellowship-affirming thing, so keep your tone upbeat.

Openness to replies and unexpected inquiries

Allow your buddy to respond and inquire. Be patient if your buddy needs a minute to repeat what you've said.

Give them a lot of twinkles to respond to, and tell them they may ask whatever questions they want.

Your pal may not have any inquiries or may state that they are not shocked.

Don't be concerned if the conversation is uncomfortable or if they don't know what to say. Allow your buddy the time they need to digest the news.

Sacred request

Inform them that you may benefit from their assistance as you reach out to others. Knowing you're not alone and have someone to depend on might make effects far less appealing.

Be honest with your pal and tell them you might need their help with your coming out vacation.

"It's such a relief that you've been so welcoming," you say. "I'm also nervous about telling other people, and I'm hoping you would be able to give me a little chat now and also. Knowing that I'm not alone in this would help me feel better about telling others."

When you come out to friends and family, you may not get the support you expected.

However, if they respond negatively, don't be disheartened. If someone needs more time to think about what you've stated. Other people can provide you with the assistance you require.

System of assistance

If you're about to tell your family, put together a support network. Coming out to your friends might help you gain confidence in yourself. If you're not sure how your parents will react, it's also crucial to have individuals you trust who can provide emotional and practical support.

Also, if you're a minor or rely on your parents for assistance, you may want to postpone coming out if you think they'll stop supporting you.

In addition, make plans to stay with a trustworthy friend or relative in case you feel compelled to inform your parents of the development.

Having support mechanisms in place might assist you in planning how to leave (

or not). Support systems can also assist you if the reactions to your coming out are not what you expected, or if you require an emergency sanctum.

Finally, make it clear to your pals that your family is unaware, and encourage them to respect your wishes if you aren't ready to inform your parents.

Big Call (Chapter 4) (Coming Out to Your Parents)

Make a drawing.

Try to predict how your parents will respond. The best-case scenario is that they will be completely welcoming, as they may have already known, and that this dialogue will not be rushed.

Coming out to your parents may also be risky, especially if they have a history of homophobic and/or transphobic behavior.

Remember that, while your parents may be accepting or have LGBTQ friends, they may react angrily when you tell them.

First and foremost, safety.

If your safety is jeopardized, don't come out. Unfortunately, there are some situations in which you would be better off not coming out to your parents.

If they have expressed homophobic and/or transphobic views, and you are financially dependent on them, it may be in your best interest to stay and tell them until you are independent.

Consider whether they will withdraw their support, stop paying for your academy education, or kick you out of the house. While it may be difficult to keep it to yourself, you should not come out to them if your safety is jeopardized.

Let go of your expectations.

People you approach may not respond in the way you expect. You'll probably find that some connections take some time to return to normal.

Some people may have lasting transformations. Friends, family members, and even the most supportive parents may need some adjustment time to adjust to your news.

Indeed, there is no assurance that your parents will respond positively to your news. Every parent answers based on their understanding.

Prior notification.

Inform close friends and family that you are about to come out to your parents (in this case, your trusted friends).

Whether your parents respond positively or negatively, it's comforting to know you have friends on whom you can rely.

However, inform them if you intend to come out to your parents and if you have previously come out to friends or cousins. Your loving family members will be there for you to vent about how things are going with your parents.

Also, ask a supportive loved one if you can stay with them if things with your parents go south. If you come out to your parents while upset, they will be concerned.

Maintain proper decorum.

Come out to your parents at a calm, relaxed time and place. Choose a time when neither you nor your parents are stressed, busy, or distracted. You may also find it easier if no major life events are approaching. For example, avoid informing them if a relative has just died or the night before your family's wedding.

This information requires your parents' complete attention. So make sure you select a time that will not be interrupted and a location that seems comfortable to you.

You're in command of the situation, and it's critical that you feel as at ease as possible. There may also be "the ideal moment" today, and if there is, you may lose your whim-whams and let the opportunity pass - that's good, don't sweat it and try again.

Ascertain that the emotional atmosphere at home is steady. If your parents are arguing or you've just been fired, you may want to remain for the effects to settle.

There are no wildcards.

Don't come out in the middle of a quarrel. You may be tempted to come out amid a fight with your parents, but you should avoid using the news as a weapon.

If you inform them you're pregnant, it will be more difficult for them to accept your choice or gender identity.

Remind them of honesty.

Tell your parents that you love them and want to be truthful with them. Begin by informing them that you want an open and loving connection with them.

Tell them how much you value their love and support and how much you want them to be a part of your life. Take a deep breath and maintain your composure.

If you're worried that they'll respond poorly, your parents may surprise you and praise you for being open. Maintain a cheerful attitude and tell them, "I'm homosexual," or "I'm bisexual," in straightforward, matter-of-fact words.

Demonstrate comprehension.

If they are astonished or scared, let them know you understand. Even the most accommodating of parents may be taken aback by your announcement.

They can be terrified that you'll have a more difficult life, or that you won't be able to marry and have children. Their anxieties may or may not be valid, but try to be empathetic rather than confrontational.

"I understand that this is a lot to take in, and you have a right to have strong passions, but this is who I am, and I'm pleased with it. This isn't a terrible thing, so please don't be upset or condemn yourself. This has nothing to do with you or your motherhood," try saying.

Assure them that you are happy and healthy, and that life presents obstacles to everyone, regardless of their gender identity or exposure.

Remind them that people are becoming more tolerant of different lifestyles in general...

Please be patient.

Allow your parents time to process the news. Parents sometimes know and are probative. Accepting the news might take months or years for some parents; regrettably, some aren't ready to accept it. Be patient and ready to answer any questions they may have.

Make sure you feel protected while you wait for them to utilize your news. The terrain may feel tense and unsettling, but as long as you're safe, you can stay at home.

While you wait for your parents to process this information, save it for your friends. Spending more time with your support network can assist you in getting through a difficult time with your parents.

Be instructive.

Suggest educational funds that could help their businesses. If your parents are initially opposed to education, they may eventually change their minds.

Try not to begin with vocabulary that is beyond their comprehension. Simply put some money aside for the parents of LGBTQ people.

There is no haste.

Bring your extended family out at your speed. When you come out to your parents, tell them you plan to come out to the rest of your family on your terms.

If you don't want other cousins to know, however, ask your parents to admire your seclusion. Take note that you have complete control over when and how you come out to the people in your life.

Of course, it's forfeiture if you believe telling other family members would be less stressful for your parents. You're in charge, so go in the direction that feels the most natural to you.

5th Chapter: Coming Out on Your Terms

Know yourself

Work on coming to terms with your gender identity. However, you might have an easier time telling your friends and family, If you're comfortable with who you are.

It's normal to feel confused, so don't feel like you need to have all of the answers. Just try to accept that your fornication or gender identity is part of who you are, and know that you have no reason to feel ashamed.

Coming out to yourself can be tough, but it's an important first step. Tell yourself, "I'm gay," "I'm bisexual," "I'm ambisexual," or "I'm questioning right now, and that's okay. I've no reason to feel shamefaced or shamed."

Reminding yourself that you're not alone can help. Try reading books or online papers about other people's coming out peregrinations.

No pressure

Bear in mind that you're in charge of your coming out process. Noway let anyone pressure you into coming out. don't let a friend or sibling press you into telling your parents, or allow a loved one to pressure you into coming out at work or the academy. You're in control of whom you tell and when, so take each step of your trip at your own pace.

You may have friends who came out a time ago, but that doesn't mean you need to follow their timelines. What's right for them isn't inescapably what's right for you.

Coming out can lift a heavy weight off of your shoulders, and it can help you feel closer to probative loved ones. Also, it can be perilous. You should not feel like coming out is your only choice, especially if you don't feel safe doing so.

Define yourself by and for yourself

Don't let others label your decision or gender identity. Borrow a marker, similar to "gay" or "bisexual" once you're comfortable with it.

However, don't let someone additional define it for you If you're doubtful or aren't ready to put a marker on your exposure or identity. Keep in mind you might feel pressure to borrow a marker from both straight and LGBTQ friends.

For illustration, suppose you tell your friend that you suppose you're bisexual, and they say, "Well I'm sure you're gay, but you're more comfortable saying 'bi' for now." No one knows you better than you and, indeed if your friend is right, no one can force you to borrow one marker or another.

An LGBTQ friend might tell you that you need to tell everyone in your life your specific exposure or gender marker to be your authentic tone. No one, whether they're homophobic or LGBTQ, has the right to mandate another person's sexual exposure or gender identity.

Being gay, bi or queer is only part of your identity, just as a straight person isn't purely defined by their sexual exposure. You don't need to change who you're to fit anyone's norms or conceptions.

Know your support system

Get a sense of how accepting a loved one is before telling them. Do your best to ensure the first person you tell is open, accepting, and supportive.

Try bringing up issues with friends and family like gay marriage or ambisexual teen homelessness, or mention an LGBTQ movie or television character.

You could say, "I saw a story on the news about same-sex marriage. What are your studies on it?"

Before you come out to someone, suppose about how accepting they're of other people. Do they have a loved one who's openly LGBTQ, and do they treat that loved one with love, support, and respect? Do they make obnoxious jokes or disparaging commentary?

Also, they might be the best person to tell first, If you have a trusted friend who's a member of the LGBTQ community. They've been in your shoes, and there's a lower threat that they'll reply negatively.

Prioritize respect

Come out to people who'll admire your sequestration. The first people you tell should be secure. When you come out to them, make it clear that they should not tell anybody about your compliments.

Before coming out to someone, consider if they are likely to agree with and accept your choice. Have they ever betrayed your faith in history? Do they reveal other people's secrets to you?

Remember that you have choices.

If writing a letter feels less frightening, do so. However, if coming out to a loved one face-to-face is too scary, or if you're terrified of being linguistically challenged, you may send them a letter instead.

Begin by telling them you trust them and wish to share vital goods with them. Also, inform them about your sexual orientation or gender identity in plain ways.

For example, you may write, "I've wanted to tell you that I'm homosexual for a little while now, but I've been so scared; I think part of me has known my whole life, but I've never accepted it until recently."

Make careful not to deliver the letter to your loved one at school, work, or in a busy area.

You could either ask them to read it privately or hand it to them and ask them to read it in your presence. It could be simpler to start the debate if you write down what you want to say.

If you're worried about coming out to your parents, writing a letter might be a helpful solution.

Conclusion (Chapter 6)

Coming out might be more difficult for teenagers who rely on their parents or other adults for their care and well-being.

Some people who come out live in areas where they are welcomed as LGBTQ. They are more likely to get assistance from family and friends. Everyone should think about their position. Everyone's situation is unique.

Do not feel compelled to come out by friends or circumstances. Coming out takes time. People are ready for it at various points in their life.

You may want to be open about your identity, but you must also consider your safety. However, it's probably safest not to participate if there's a risk of being physically injured or thrown out of the home.

Weigh all of your options and ask yourself, "How can coming out make my life more delicate? How would it make effects easier? Is it worth it?"

Make it happen if all or most of the questions are answered.